Religion

vs.

Relationship

By Mary Ellen

Do you know the difference and how would you describe your connection to God?

Brother / Sister in Christ,

As you enter into this journey, be honest with yourself. Take an honest look at your everyday Christian life. We can lie to others and we can lie to ourselves, but we cannot lie to God. Even if we choose to deny truth, Father knows long before we do. You cannot change what you will not accept or do not acknowledge. Perhaps a better way to say it is, just because you don't like the truth does not make it any less the truth. It is my fervent prayer that we will all grow; reach that next level, not only during this next several days but every day beyond that. May your heart grow closer to our Lord and your hunger to know Him and be in His presence get ever stronger, 'til we all go home.

Mary Ellen

Dedication

I want to dedicate this study and the inspiration for it to my precious, my daughter Chassity. I am thankful for her prayers and gently nudging her momma when she saw room for growth. Her desire that I have and develop a true relationship with the Lord has planted a seed that the Holy Spirit is still developing, and I am forever humbled and grateful for her insight.

Thank you for understanding my heart and knowing how to help me be what I longed to be, where I longed to be.

Thank you, my precious baby girl.

Momma

Foundation

The question, to myself and anyone that calls themselves a child of God is – do you truly know the difference between an honest relationship and the practice of religion? Unfortunately, I would venture to say that many have never even considered the two as separate. We don't necessarily grow up with the understanding that God is our friend and confidant – not many of us anyway. In growing up, my circle of influence and understanding would tend toward a heavenly God that is almost abstract. You are taught to fear his wrath because judgment is coming. You see understanding that all prayers are heard but hear some speak of "deserving" blessings or earning God's favor. It is not something that we readily recognize or would even think to look for.

Here is the problem, if consider our religion to be a relationship rather than our relationship to be our religion – we are one step away from falling without a net at all times. God is first and foremost our Father, He is our Creator and He has a father's heart. What we need to truly contemplate is, do we have a child's heart, child like faith, and what kind of child are we?

Let's spend some time together looking at the difference between religion and relationship, some of which are very subtle. We will look at relationships in the Bible that can help us develop and maintain a good connection with God. In taking a closer look, we can learn to build, and build, and build a healthy relationship with our Father. A connection that will strengthen with time.

Section 1

What is your definition of a relationship?

How would you define a relationship? We have many different kinds in our lives. We have friends, relatives, co-workers and buddies. Our relationship with our spouse is not the same as that which we have with our siblings, for example. So... to define the concept of relationship rather than let it be subjective, let's look at dictionary.com.

It is defined as *an association or connection. It can be defined by blood or marriage. It is also an emotional or other connection between two people.* This last defining characteristic is the one we need to zero in on. To have a connection with the Lord, especially an emotional connection or bond, is to have a relationship with the Lord.

Proverbs 18:24 says we have a friend that sticks closer than a brother, but do we treat him as that close friend? Okay... so, let's put it into every day perspective. How do you, personally, define a relationship with others? This will help you redefine your relationship with our Father. We have our parents, siblings, spouses and children. This is the family bond. This is an emotional bond that transcends anger, offense, time and distance. You *feel* the connection no matter where you are, and they are usually only a thought or two away from whatever you are doing at that moment. Some of our friends are even that close to our hearts. It is not the same as with a neighbor or co-worker. Those relationships while important don't have the same type of emotional bond. Ask yourself which type of relationship you have with God. Is it that familial, best friend bond that is life altering if absent or removed? Or, is it the neighbor you visit with over the fence once a week or so? You care and if he went away it would hurt your feelings, but it wouldn't impact or alter your everyday life.

Second point, how do you know the difference? Are there specific characteristics that specifically separate the types of relationships in your eyes? An example might be in weighing one against the other. Take your absolute best friend and make note of the emotion attached. It doesn't matter if that BFF is your parent, sibling, spouse or buddy. Now, think about the person in the closest chair to you at work – not your BFF if they work in the same place of course. Do you have similar emotions? If both were suddenly removed from your life, what would the impact be?

In Genesis you will find the retelling of creation and God's faith speaking us into existence. You will also find a very important point in God's nature. It happens to be something near and dear to my heart. Genesis 3:8 tells us they heard the voice of the Lord as he was walking in the garden in the cool of the evening. Now, he didn't just suddenly decide to come to the garden and see. I believe it is an indication of the relationship he had with Adam and perhaps Eve. He very much wants to have the same relationship with each of us. We can facilitate this if we would just hear him and respond. Come out from behind the trees!

Adam's relationship with God would appear to be one of trust and confidence. He loved God or why would he have hidden? Yes, the scripture tells us that Adam did not want God to see his nakedness but, he wasn't hiding from Eve. He wasn't worried about Eve seeing him in the same state of "undress". Did they not make coverings – sort of. I must wonder, was Adam hiding in guilt and shame or was it fear? I would suggest he had an emotional bond with the Lord. He had to know God was going to be disappointed and/or mad. He had done the one thing God had said not to do. The scriptures do not actually outline their relationship, I am speculating to an extent, but I can tell you how I would feel. God only told me to NOT do the ONE thing and THAT is the very thing I did! We do see that God did not separate Himself from them completely because we see in Cain and Abel's lives, they are interacting with the Lord. It may not be on the same level, as they are no longer in the garden, but He did not leave them.

A relationship is defined by the level of commitment or dedication held by the two parties involved. A relationship is never supposed to be a one-way street. A relationship can define your very existence as well as the other person's. How strong that relationship is depends entirely on how strong you want to make it. How easy that relationship is depends on how strong you want to make it. How much that relationship blesses you, depends on how invested you are in it. Your relationship with the Lord depends entirely on how invested you are in it and how strong you want to make it.

A relationship knows the Father and not just his gifts or blessings. A relationship loves the Father and not just the muscle he flexes in your protection. A relationship is built on mutual respect and trust and love. A relationship reciprocates feelings and emotional investment. Mother always said, you get out of everything, exactly what you put into it.

Discovery:

1. If God was completely removed from your life right now.... What would be different?

    _____

    _____

    _____

2. Would you miss <u>Him,</u> or would you miss <u>His promises</u>?

    _____

    _____

    _____

3. Do you know Him, or do you know about Him?

    _____

    _____

    _____

4. If you had to characterize your relationship with the Lord, would you say it is as close as the one you have with your closest companion or more like the checkout person at the grocery store?

_____

_____

_____

5. What can you do today to change the answers you don't like?

_____

_____

_____

Personal Application/Discovery Journal

_____

_____

_____

_____

_____

_____

I have a relationship with Jesus.

I am not religious

Section 2

How do you define religion? Hosea 5:6

We know this turn of phrase or commonly used identifier. The first thing that comes to mind is that it is widely used to describe or label any practice of any faith. Also coming to mind is that it is commonly used to be excused from something, "it's against my religion". The dictionary.com definition is *"the belief in and worship of a superhuman controlling power, especially a personal God or gods"*. I am not fond of this definition, mostly because of the religious concept in its wording; however, it kind of makes the point for me. I must say though, God is not a supernatural controlling power; if He had complete control then the world would not be broken and dying. As it is, He gave us authority here and we can choose to submit to His authority... glory to God!

Back to our point; unfortunately, supernatural controlling power is how many see the Lord because they don't know Him on a personal level. I absolutely mean personal just like you and I talking or having coffee. Religion is the practice of acting like we know the Lord. I think the best way to truly convey the concept is by example.

My first example would be church attendance. Some of us are there every time the doors are open for just about anything. Others among us are there for scheduled worship service. And when it comes to the difference between religion and relationship, either one could in fact be the truth. Your attendance doesn't change your relationship with the Lord, your heart does. Let me be careful here, church attendance is unquestionably vital to a Christian's spiritual wellbeing. The Lord says to be careful and make sure we attend, especially in the last days as we see His time approaching. *Heb 10:25* HOWEVER, attendance by itself is not an indicator of your relationship. Religion attends church service for the sake of attending service, it's the thing you do. Relationship attends the church service only for the Lord, to serve the Lord and be in his presence. It is a purposeful attendance. It is easy to fall into the habit of attending and the work of serving; we must work to guard against the enemy robbing us of the joy of being in the Lord's house. It is after all for the Lord, not your pastor.

My next example would be our study or prayer time. Where is your heart and focus when you approach that time with the Lord?

Is it a joyous, let's have coffee time or is it more of an obligation to be filled? It's like you can earn some measure of blessing or wisdom if you maintain the strict practice of prayer and bible time. As if you were saying - I have to spend at least 30 minutes today or I just haven't studied at all. Then we set a timer and check it every 10 minutes to see if we are done yet.

Let me paint a picture for you... consider you and your child going to the grandparent's house to visit. You of course have a good relationship with them. It is easy to sit and drink coffee, tea or a soda and catch up. You are invested in what happened to them and they are invested in what has happened recently in your life. Your teen spends their time on the couch or in the chair – on the cell, checking social media. Maybe even posting about how they are visiting with their grandparents. When the visit is concluded, you get up, say your goodbyes and everyone leaves. You have connected with the parents and the teen got in some tweets about #grandparentsaregreat. You acted on your relationship and built it stronger. The teen was simply along for the ride. They can tell you what was discussed. They will talk about visiting the grandparents and how they love them but there was no connection made, no period of bonding. That is religion. It is an outward behavior or exhibition of practice that is lacking the meat of true connection.

In truth, in regards to the Lord, religion is a state of mind and heart. It is the "why" that is driving you and not the "what" you are doing? It doesn't really matter how many examples I can bring, they will all boil down to the same question. Why are you doing it? What is your motivation? What are you investing in the bond? Did you make a connection? I guess that is more than one question but... you get the point.

So here is my question for you.... If you were to be quizzed about it, how would you characterize yourself? If you are honest and truly look at your practices and service, do you see religious practice or relational fellowship?

Discovery:

1. Can you go before the Lord and ask him to reveal areas of your life that are more religion than relationship? It takes courage.

    _____

    _____

    _____

2. If you are honest, can you identify areas of religious practice in your life?

    _____

    _____

    _____

3. What is your motivation to attend church on Sunday morning/Wednesday evening?

    _____

    _____

    _____

4. How can you enrich your time with the Lord today?

    _____

_____

_____

5. Are you prepared to move forward in your
    relationship and explode with God?

    _____

    _____

    _____

6. Are there any changes you think you could
    make to invest yourself more personally?

    _____

    _____

    _____

Personal Application/Discovery Journal

_____

_____

_____

_____

_____

_____

Section 3

Why do you do the things you do?

1Sa 16:7 *But the LORD said unto Samuel, Look not on his countenance, or on the height of his stature; because I have refused him: for the LORD seeth not as man seeth; for man looketh on the outward appearance, but the LORD looketh on the heart.*

Let's continue with our discussion on motivation. You see, God is so much more interested in our hearts than our actions – truthfully. We can do all the right things for the wrong reasons and make them wrong. Our motivation relects our heart and our driving force.

So, what is your motivation for anything you do for the Lord? That is a question we should each ask ourselves every time we step out to serve or participate in any capacity. Okay, so perhaps, every time would be a little extreme, but you get my point.

Are you reading your Bible out of a sense of task driven compliance, like it is a chore that you want to do but a chore all the same? Are you praying because you think you HAVE to pray a certain amount of time each day? Are your prayers scripted because you HAVE to use certain words? Are you at church every service because someone might notice you gone and think less of you? Or out of responsibility or obligation to your leadership? What I want to say to you today is the motivation behind what you are doing and where you are going makes all the difference in the world in what you will walk away with. You will notice I used the words CHORE and HAVE to. Now, for a moment consider your grown children coming to visit and only doing so because they HAVE to. Or visiting because it is a chore to mark off of their responsibility check list, one they enjoy but it feels like a chore anyway. I don't want anyone to ever spend time with me or visit with me out of some sort of obligation and I don't believe for a moment that our Heavenly Father does either. There is no free will in the bondage of HAVE to. His blessings can't be purchased. You can't earn His love, it is a gift freely given and freely to be received.

Let's also look at another facet of motivation, personal gain. If walking this Christian life in HAVE to mode is bad, then pursuing the things of God or serving in any capacity for personal gain is ten times worse. When we start doing things in order for others to "see" how holy we are, how obedient we are or anything at all we are... then we have moved over to where Jesus found much of the Israeli leadership. We wouldn't notice it, but we are right in line with those that wore sack cloth and ashes when they were fasting and garnered attention. You know, so everyone knew they were making a sacrifice before God. Or those that prayed and would stand on street corners and pray loudly and quite long with million-dollar words and prayers that sounded like they were constructed for formal treatises. *Matthew 6:1-5* paints a picture of wrong motivation and Jesus warns us against it. We don't see the correlation because we aren't making a spectacle of ourselves but is the condition of the heart really that much different?

Wrong motivation will also open the door to satan's interference and corrupt whatever you are trying to accomplish. It is very important that we are careful and examine our drive before we kick it into gear.

Honestly, I would suggest that the only right motivation for doing anything in God's kingdom is for His honor and for His glory, to spread His good news and preach Christ. We are either fighting to save those that are lost, or we are striving to be the hands and feet of the Lord so others can see His true heart.

Discovery:

1. Take an honest look at your "why" for the things you do every day in relation to God, what do you see?

_____

_____

_____

2. If you were on the receiving end, would your motivation be acceptable to you?

_____

_____

_____

3. Even if the motivation was honest and right before you started, is it still?

_____

_____

_____

4. Have you asked the Lord to reveal to you any hidden agenda you have not recognized?

_____

_____

_____

5. Is love for God at the heart of your effort?

_____

_____

_____

Personal Application/Discovery Journal

_____

_____

_____

_____

Section 4

Exo 20:2 I am the LORD thy God, which have brought thee out of the land of Egypt, out of the house of bondage.

If you look at the dictionary definition of real this is what you will find *"actually existing as a thing or occurring in fact; not imagined or supposed"*. So, my question for you would be, is God actually existing and a fact; not imagined or supposed in your heart? Most of us would immediately, without hesitation, exclaim and insist God is real to us. However, in your heart we see Him as more of an abstract reality. That all-knowing and all-powerful Creator of Heaven and Earth that lives way off somewhere and we are seemingly insignificant to His royal majesty. That is not real to you, that is accepting that He exists and no real experience of His person.

Moses at the point in his life when God met him by the burning bush knew God existed but in that moment, God became as real to him as the rocks he was standing on. From *Exodus 3:1-6,* we know Moses knew who God was. As he grew up in the Egyptian household, because his own mother was his nurse maid, I am sure Jehovah God was discussed on some level. As a child in Pharaoh's house God would have been referred to in some manner as the God of the Hebrews. It was at this point, *Exod 3:1-6,* that Moses could not deny His reality in existence, though I am not suggesting he did not know Him before. I am stating that at this point, there was no option for denial of His reality. In that moment Moses came face to face with the Almighty. Many of us would say that would make us believe too. It would, at least for a time. Even now, many of us can tell of an experience of God, where His presence was unmistakable. It was great and awesome and the further in days we get away from it, the less we remember it, let alone allow it to impact our perception.

Moses walked with the Lord as his close companion for the rest of his days. As you read through the scriptures you see the results of that. Evidenced in the deliverance of Israel from Egypt, which was the purpose in Father calling Moses to service. The books of the law go over all that the Lord gave us through Moses. Moses had a bond with the Lord. He depended on God to lead him and Israel through the wilderness. Moses knew God was the protector and provider. Moses knew God's heart. God was larger than life in Moses' life and days.

Even if you or I had a burning bush experience, would we dedicate ourselves to Him as Moses did? Would we follow up that connection with further investment of ourselves? Moses may not be a good example as he was on assignment but, every one of us is on assignment too. We may not have a nation of Egypt to help God overcome but for someone, you might be Moses that helps them escape their personal Egypt. If you look at *Matthew 28:19*, you will see that Jesus has called each of us to be Moses or

Jesus to the lost and hurting of this world. You can do that, even if it is just one person at a time.

When you sit down to pray, do you believe He is listening? What is your perception of prayers and how they "travel"? When you sit down to pray, do you believe that Jesus sits down next to you to listen? Is that in real time or do you think it is more like sending a letter and He will read it later? In honesty, I think this question alone will help you answer the questions for this section. When Moses called out to God, did God not answer? Did Moses wait for days, weeks and months to "hear" back? The answer is no, he didn't wait. It was a delicate and important operation God had invited Moses to partner with Him on and they were not finished until Israel had made it to the Promised Land.

You are no less important to God, our Father, than Israel was. Our problem is much like that of the children of Israel – He is not always REAL to us. How quickly they lost hope and faith and spoke against God when they didn't think they were being provided for fast enough. How quickly they grumbled and griped in the days of travel. How long will God let us suffer? Did He deliver us from Egypt only to let us die of thirst or hunger in the wilderness? God was not a reality to them, not as He was to Moses and even on some level to Aaron, let's not leave out Aaron who helped Moses.

Are you like that? When you don't see progress or the answer in what you consider due time, do you start doubting and questioning and grumbling? Of course you do, so do I and many others – at one point or another. Our problem is that we have lost that contact or connection and perhaps got too focused on the "what" and neglected the Who of our desires or needs.

The relationship version of this scenario is to say that God is very real to each of us. To know and understand that our love for Him and His love and concern for us is mutual and ever growing, is to be in a relationship. When we do not have ready answers, we do not question His will or doubt His promise, but we look for His leading. What is God teaching me? What is God preparing either for me or in me? What would God have me to be doing right now, in this season of waiting?

The religious answer to this is very much different. Religion would suggest that it must not be, after all, God would have done something by now. It's a "sign" of God's will that I do not have an answer. Religion suggests you didn't pray enough, you didn't give enough or were not "good" enough to deserve the desire of your heart. Religion suggests that God must have something better for me. My all-time least favorite, I guess it is not meant to be. The key words being must have, sign, would have, should have and I guess.

Discovery:

1. Where do you think God can be found when you set down to pray?

   _____

   _____

   _____

2. Do you believe that God is listening, at all times and to all His children?

   _____

   _____

   _____

3. Have you ever had a burning bush moment in your life?

   _____

   _____

   _____

   a. What did you do with that connection?

      _____

      _____

      _____

4. If you had to describe how real God is to you in your every day life, how would you do that?

_____

_____

_____

5. Do you think God could ever be as real a
    presence in your life as He was to those
    men and women who walked with Him in
    the Bible – if He isn't now of course?

    _____

    _____

    _____

Personal Application/Discovery Journal

_____

_____

_____

_____

_____

_____

_____

Section 5

What is in your God box?

Mar 8:29 *And he saith unto them, But whom say ye that I am? And Peter answereth and saith unto him, Thou art the Christ.*

In other words, what defines your relationship with God – in your eyes, who is He to you? What elements or building blocks are present to define your relationship with Father God? Let me explain a bit because we don't want anyone putting God in a box, in fact we very much would like Him taken out of said religious box.

I keep what I call memory boxes. They contain pictures, favorite pieces of clothing and mementos of those represented. I only have a few and mostly they belong to loved ones that have entered their eternity. This box represents them in my life. The items within are memories we shared or things that speak to me of them. If you consider it, I would like to think that every relationship has what we could call a content box that defines it or is the foundation for the relationship. It could hold the elements that make up that relationship. There is no standard for what should be in the "box", but the contents are what define the investment you make emotionally and personally. It could hold your memories with and of them. It could hold the building blocks for that relationship. My daughter box, for example, would have the parental bond and unconditional love in it. It also might contain respect, a mutual love for God and ministry, fondness for all things Star related (think movies and television) even to one that travels in space and time, relatively of course. My brother and sister boxes are similar in that they might contain the all forgiving and unconditional love that is developed through sharing life together as siblings. It also contains the family bond of heritage and memories of people, places and events from passing years. There is also the respect and concern for their wellbeing. The things we shared with each other or with one of our parents. It could contain items that represented the things we have in common. I think you get the idea. So, if you were to look for it... what is in your God box?

If you were to unpack your box and take inventory, what would your list look like? The "inventory" of your box will identify the level or type of relationship you have with our Heavenly Father. Only you can identify what is in your "God box". It will also tell you what you believe might be missing and what you could work on to strengthen and deepen that connection. Is the relationship one sided? Is it a list that is mainly His giving to you and His doing for you? Does it contain a mutual investment and love?

John, in the book of Revelation, has given us an idea as to what to look for in our box and helps us identify where our connection to the Lord could be lacking, or weak. There are letters to the churches, the body of Christ, starting in chapter 2. You can go through each letter and see what is identified to John as missing or lacking – is that in your box? Or is it also missing in you? I regularly go over these letters to the churches and ask God to help me identify anything in my life that is not what it should be. **1Cor 11:31** *"For if we would judge ourselves, we should not be judged."* Is there a prayer "book" in your box and is it a small one or a large volume? Is there a study calendar or schedule, how full is it? Will you find tools for service in your box and how many? Will you find obedience to His word? How about compassion for the lost and hurting? Are you happy with the contents?

Discovery:

1. Make a list of those things that you believe should be in your God box?

   _____

   _____

   _____

2. Make a list of the items that you know are in your God box?

   _____

   _____

   _____

3. What do you identify as missing?

   _____

   _____

Personal Application/Discovery Journal

_____

_____

_____

_____

_____

_____

_____

_____

_____

_____

_____

_____

_____

_____

_____

_____

_____

Section 6

Side by side comparison...

It is extremely unwise to regularly compare yourself to another when considering your relationship with Christ or your Christian walk on any level. Actually, I wouldn't suggest ever comparing yourself with anyone other than Christ himself. Comparing yourself to others is like comparing an original you with a copy of God, it just doesn't work. However, for the sake of teaching, let's take a look at some men from the scriptures and their relationship with God, or lack thereof. Much like I suggest we do with the letters to the churches in Revelation, compare yourself and your habits to each of them as we go through this.

Cain and Abel

I want to start, well, at the beginning. We have two brothers, seemingly on even ground. Each of the two were the second generation of man, or children of Adam and Eve. We see in Genesis 4, after the garden was closed off to us, that children were born. These two men would have sat at their parent's feet or knees and listened to firsthand accounts of God and his mercy. This story telling, or retelling is how information and history was passed down from generation to generation. We also know that giving God an offering was a practice for them both.

Gen 4:3 - 5 *And in process of time it came to pass, that Cain brought of the fruit of the ground an* *offering unto the LORD. And Abel, he also brought of the firstlings of his flock and of the fat thereof. And the LORD had respect unto Abel and to his offering: But unto Cain and to his offering he had not respect. And Cain was very wroth, and his countenance fell.*

Each of them had an opportunity to give to God and easily could both have received the same response from Father in turn. The difference was the respect or fear of God held in each heart. The verses tell the story. Cain brought of the fruit of his labors, it is not specific in description. There is not a telling of the first fruits or the choice fruits or the best fruits... just fruits. Abel on the other hand is a better presentation. Abel brought of his firstlings and the fat, which you could also say the richest or best part. Abel brought God his firsts.

There are two things here that are important to point out. First, is the respect mentioned, it says God had no respect for Cain or his offering. How many times have we brought something before the Lord that wasn't our best and then knew in our hearts that we had done wrong, probably before we gave it. We know, the Holy Spirit ministers that to us, we just choose to hear or not to hear. Would it surprise any of us to hear God tell us He doesn't respect our offering if it is not our best? Second is Cain's response to God's lack of acceptance. He got very mad and it even showed in him physically. I must say I too would be hurt or upset. What really tells the condition of Cain's heart is how he responds to it. You see, God warns him, tells him what to guard against and how to be right before the Lord. But Cain's answer or response to this was to eliminate the competition. He murdered Abel who had found favor in God's eyes rather than change how he handled himself.

There isn't much here on Abel. Abel brought his first and his best to the Lord, it was acceptable in God's eyes and Abel moved on. Cain is our source of learning here, because in such a short telling a great deal happened. Cain brought what he wanted to before the Lord rather than what was honorable. We know that based on God's reaction. Cain refused correction as God made it plain and simple – if you do well, won't it be accepted and if you do not then sin lies in wait to overtake you. *(Gen 4:7)* Then Cain eliminated the comparison, I surmise in jealousy, perhaps thinking it would make his offering look better. The verses don't tell us, but I can imagine there may have been an argument; after all, Cain was angry enough to kill Abel.

Abel loved God enough to honor him and put him first – this is born of relationship. Cain was only doing what had to be done to get the task completed – definition of religious practice.

Discovery:

1. With whom do you identify most?

_____

_____

_____

    a. Why?

_____

_____

_____

2. Are you happy with what you have discovered?

_____

_____

_____

3. Looking back, we have 20/20 vision... can you take an honest look at your "right now" and see the "negatives" within your daily walk?

_____

_____

_____

4. If you find one, what is your greatest obstacle to overcome at this point?

_____

_____

_____

5. What steps do you think you should take to remove those "negative" like identifiers and overcome your obstacle?

_____

_____

_____

Personal Application/Discovery Journal

_____

_____

_____

_____

_____

_____

_____

_____

_____

_____

_____

_____

_____

_____

_____

_____

_____

David and Saul

David and Saul are our next comparison. Each man was chosen by God to be king of Israel. Saul had the honor of being the first ever to wear the crown. God sent Samuel to each of them, to find and anoint them king. Each was far from having notions of ruling a country. Saul was chasing his father's donkeys when Samuel found him. David was tending his father's sheep when Samuel came in search of him.

Again, each man started out on the same level ground, one did not have an advantage over the other. The difference lies in their hearts and how they treated God's role in their rule.

Saul started out well enough. He would take direction from the Lord as Samuel brought it to him. However, he started to slowly move more toward Saul controlling things rather than obeying God's instruction. Specifically, in one instance Saul was waiting on Samuel to come and offer a sacrifice before the Lord, so that Israel could go into battle. Saul became very impatient and performed the sacrifice himself, so he could move on with his plans. This took God out of the equation. This was about Saul's timing rather than waiting on God's timing. Saul was focused on going to battle right now, so they could win rather than trusting in God's strength to conquer the enemy. This became a practice or consistent thing for Saul. He repeatedly disobeyed God's instructions; he was even warned and still insisted on doing things his way. Saul wanted God's blessing and protection as well as his strength and power, but didn't want to submit to God's leadership.

David was said, by God, to be a man after God's own heart. God specifically said to Saul that he had found one that would do as he asked him to. Someone that would be obedient. David was not perfect, but he loved God and was obedient in all matters that God instructed him on. He only went to battle when God advised him to. He accepted God's instructions wholeheartedly. We can even go a step further and say that from the beginning, David always gave God the glory. From the day of his battle with Goliath, you see a man that knows that it is God's enemy, Israel's enemy and not his own personally. You also see a man willing to protect what he knows is God's, right down to sparing Saul's life and even avenging his death because he was anointed by God to be king. Many of us, once we had been anointed, would have forgotten or set to the side the fact that our predecessor had been chosen king by the same hand. Would we have protected the one trying to kill us? David spared Saul's life more than once because of God's anointing him. That is the main difference between the two... their heart for God's heart.

Saul chased his own agenda and wanted God to bless and empower him to do so. I am sure Saul saw himself as God's king doing God's work, but Saul tried to do it in his own power more than God's anointing. If he had trusted God, he wouldn't have been in a hurry to have the offering done and completed, so he could get to battle. Saul did not know God's heart, just his name.

David wanted God's will to be done over all and was willing to do whatever the Lord asked of him. What is more, he wasn't willing to reduce or destroy anything that God had put his name or hand on. David protected Saul, saying on more than one occasion that Saul was anointed of God and it was not for him to kill him, but for God. David even protected or avenged God's man after his death when the servant reported he had slain Saul in battle. For David, Saul's death was not such a victory as much as a loss of God's anointed. He didn't see the man trying to kill him for so many years, he saw God's chosen. David knew God's heart and put it above all else.

Discovery:

1. With whom do you identify most?

_____

_____

_____

   a. Why?

_____

_____

_____

2. Are you happy with what you have discovered?

_____

_____

_____

3. Looking back, we have 20/20 vision... can you take an honest look at your "right now" and see the "negatives" within your daily walk?

_____

_____

_____

4. If you find one, what is your greatest obstacle to overcome at this point?

_____

_____

_____

5. What steps do you think you should take to remove those "negative" like identifiers and overcome your obstacle?

_____

_____

_____

Personal Application/Discovery Journal

_____

_____

_____

_____

_____

_____

_____

_____

John vs Judas

John the Revelator, also known as the one that Jesus loved, and Judas Iscariot were two of the twelve disciples that walked with Jesus. They served with him, ate with him, traveled with him and listened to his teaching for the duration of his ministry. There are only a few instances where you see that John is part of an inner circle that witnesses Jesus in a different setting. Other than that, John and Judas would have been equally unknown to Jesus from the beginning of his ministry and his call on them to join him. Again, we start with what we can call equal footing for each man. While there is not a lot of information to compare these two men, we do have enough to make our point.

The truth of the differences in these two men, their relationship with Christ, is evident in the fruit of their lives and end of their lives rather than specific acts or moments, like we find in the previous comparisons. I chose these two because they are as opposite each other as any two disciples could have been. Each had the same access to Jesus teaching in more intimate settings than the general populous. Each man had the same opportunities to learn, grow and serve in the kingdom. As far as being offered truth, walking in proximity, hearing the Messiah and living in the Lord's shadow, they each had the same exposure.

The differences are in the men's hearts and choices. This determined the soil that the truth of God was planted in and what kind of fruit came to bear.

John was called by Jesus along with his brother James. He had been a fisherman as were a few of the other disciples that were called. He immediately left his boat and followed Jesus. While he was not perfect, he was teachable. Despite attempts to the contrary, his life ended naturally at a good old age. He wrote several of the books of the New Testament. He helped spread the kingdom and church of God alongside the other disciples and Paul. John is known as John the Revelator, due to the book of Revelation. John's service is sprinkled all through the books of the New Testament.

Judas was called as a disciple, however, the first mentioning was in Jesus ordaining the twelve to go out and spread the gospel, and in following verses all twelve are listed (Matt 10:1-4). Except for his betrayal in the garden, there is very little mention of Judas Iscariot, if any at all. We know Jesus trusted Judas, or entrusted to Judas, the money bag for the group. We also know Judas stole from the money that was entrusted to him. That is really all that is told. The glaring difference or fruit of his life that I want to point out is his death. His life ended suddenly and tragically. While some of the disciples also had their lives taken from them suddenly, it was in service to God, as martyrs. Judas' life was not taken by others or in God's service but by his own hand. (Matt 27:4-5)

The fruit that we are comparing between these two disciples is the end of their days on earth. John enjoyed long life and supernatural protection from those that would see him destroyed. While the account of John being boiled in oil and surviving is not found in scripture, it is recorded in other historical texts. Even if you chose to remove that as heresy or hearsay, either way, you cannot deny his long life as compared to any other disciple and especially to Judas Iscariot. Judas on the other hand met a very tragic and sad end. His regret at having turned over Jesus and learning he would be crucified ended in him taking his own life.

John walked with Jesus and learned from him, knew his heart and love. Judas walked with Jesus and never truly knew his heart and held no love for him, let alone others. John's fruits are the books he wrote and his love for God. He is still touching hearts for Christ. Judas's fruit is to be remembered as the betrayer and have betrayal referenced back to him specifically. He has become synonymous with betrayal.

We have clearly seen through scripture the outcome of each man's connection to God. This enables us to easily say, I am not like that. However, if you were walking next to them... could you have said the same? Do we take to heart those things that the scripture brings to us? Do we take seriously the scriptural warnings about choosing self or the world over the Lord?

Discovery:

1. Who do you identify with most?

    _____

    _____

    _____

    a. Why?

    _____

    _____

    _____

2. Are you happy with what you have discovered?

    _____

    _____

    _____

3. Looking back, we have 20/20 vision... can you take an honest look at your "right now" and see the "negatives" within your daily walk?

    _____

    _____

    _____

4. If you find one, what is your greatest obstacle to overcome at this point?

    _____

    _____

_____

5. What steps do you think you should take to remove those "negative" like identifiers and overcome your obstacle?

_____

_____

_____

Personal Application/Discovery Journal

_____

_____

_____

_____

_____

_____

_____

_____

_____

_____

Discovery:

1. With each comparison, who do you identify most with?

   _____

   _____

   _____

   a. Was it more often the positive or relational example or the religious example?

      _____

      _____

      _____

2. Change is never easy and will not happen overnight. Are you prepared to commit to making that change to build a relationship, a stronger relationship than you have now?

   _____

   _____

   _____

Personal Application/Discovery Journal

_____

_____

_____

_____

Section 7

In Conclusion ...

John 4:24 *God is a Spirit: and they that worship him must worship him in spirit and in truth.*

TRUTH - Truth by definition is *"that which is true or in accordance with fact or reality"*. This is where we want to get – to the truth of it all. So that all we do is in a heart of worship for our King and is in TRUTH. This means it is not just actions but a true reflection of our heart. It is an extension of our love for God and not just an act of obedience, fear or sense of "you have to" out of some religious practice, so he doesn't strike you down, or withhold blessings and favor.

Jesus stated that he only did what he saw the Father do and said what he heard the Father say (John 5:19 and John 12:49). Can you say the same as Jesus? When you speak to others or about others, would your words be those of the Lord? When you go about your daily life – are your actions those that you have seen exhibited in scripture? Would the Lord easily be able to follow you, in your footsteps without stepping around sin, anger or a lack of love for His children?

Moses stepped out in faith and let God use him to lead the nation to deliverance and return to the Promised Land.

Abraham being the father of faith had such faith that it was counted to righteousness. He is the example of true belief even in the face of apparent defeat.

David was a man after God's own heart and God said David would do whatever God asked Him to. David's blessing to God was his obedience.

John truly knew the love of God in Christ and through his writings in the New Testament tries to teach us the same.

Job had unfaltering faith in the face of profound adversity. He lost everything - and then some - and still gave God praise and unfailing loyalty.

Mary had such trust that is was beyond self-preservation. She knew in receiving God's call on her life she would be ridiculed and shamed as a sinner.

Paul had such favor with God that the enemy paid for Paul's room and board while Paul taught Christ to the Roman guard and government. He was supposed to be in prison but was ministering daily to all who sought to hear the truth.

Peter was the one Jesus called the rock. Peter denied Christ three times and then became a foundation of the church. Fear caused him to sin but that didn't keep him from coming back and pushing back the enemy lines.

Stephen exhibited complete unabashed forgiveness even though he was facing his death and his killers. His last words were for those that were killing him.

All these listed here are good examples of a person seeking after and serving Christ and expanding the kingdom of God. However, they are not Christ. We can learn from them, what to do and not to do, but they are not our standard.

In seeking a relationship with Christ rather than practicing religion, I believe a valid question would be – who are you emulating? Who/what are you measuring yourself against? Are you following Christ's teachings or the teaching of the church/pastor? Are you more interested in what the word of God says or how a man has taught it? Is your concern focused on others "seeing" your service or approving your walk, or is it a concern for God's heart and kingdom?

Religion is worried and working for the church building, the practices, the events, the attendance count and the ceremonies. Relationship is worried and working for the body, the salvation of the lost, the healing of the sick, the deliverance of the bound and the liberty of all who seek God.

Religion is the habit of agreeing to pray for someone, even posting on social media the popular "prayers" or "praying". Relationship will pray and make a point of continuing to do so, accepting the responsibility of praying rather than just being part of the call to pray.

Religion puts all power, heart and purpose into the ceremony while relationship is more interested in the purpose of the ceremony. What does the "ceremony" signify? What does practice of this event mean?

Sometimes, there is a fine line between religion and relationship. It is found at the point of complacency and doing things this way "because that's the way we have always done it", because "my parents did it this way". Each of us can cross that line at any time if we are not careful.

Discovery:

1. Were you honest with yourself as you came through each section?

   _____

   _____

   _____

2. What did you find that you want to do differently?

   _____

   _____

   _____

3. What did you discover that you are pleased with?

   _____

   _____

   _____

4. What are you going to change that will bring you closer to the Lord?

_____

_____

_____

5. What are you doing with your relationship to help others develop their relationship?

_____

_____

_____

Personal Application/Discovery Journal

_____

_____

_____

_____

_____

_____

_____

Plus:

James is an excellent book if you are looking for what you might call a road map. It is a short book and very guiding, that is the word I am going to use, guiding. It is all about "how" to be a Christian. I would suggest reading it, repeatedly. I would also always suggest reading the book of Proverbs, repeatedly. There are testimonies given to attest to Proverbs literally increasing a person's intelligence after having read it over time. Either of these books are valuable resources for anybody seeking a closer walk with God. And of course... there is the rest of the book too. ☺

54332473R00030

Made in the USA
Columbia, SC
29 March 2019